also by nikki giovanni

ego-tripping

and other poems for young people

by nikki giovanni

with illustrations by

george ford

LAWRENCE HILL
AND COMPANY
New York • Westport

poems copyright © 1973 by nikki giovanni
illustrations copyright © 1973 george ford

permission to reprint the following poems:
alone, kidnap poem, the geni in the jar, 2nd rapp,
ego-tripping, poem for flora, poem for my nephew,
has been granted by broadside press, detroit, michigan.

permission to reprint the following poems:
black power, word poem, poem for black boys,
the funeral of martin luther king, jr., nikki-rosa,
intellectualism, knoxville, tennessee, has been granted by
william morrow & company, inc., new york, n.y.

library of congress catalogue card number: 73-81745
international standard book number: 0-88208-020-2
manufactured in the united states of america

library of congress
cataloging in publication data
giovanni, nikki
ego-tripping and other poems for young people
I. title.
PS3557.I55E4   811'.5'4   73-81745
ISBN 0-88208-020-2

for Lena, Nina & Ida—
very special egos to me

N.G.

and for Paul Robeson—
whose shadow is longest and tallest
and Blackest

G.F.

contents

kidnap poem

ever been kidnapped
by a poet
if i were a poet
i'd kidnap you
put you in my phrases and meter
you to jones beach
or maybe coney island
or maybe just to my house
lyric you in lilacs
dash you in the rain
blend into the beach
to complement my see
play the lyre for you
ode you with my love song
anything to win you
wrap you in the red Black green
show you off to mama
yeah if i were a poet i'd kid
nap you

17 feb. 70

1

ego-tripping
(there may be a reason why)

I was born in the congo
I walked to the fertile crescent and built
   the sphinx
I designed a pyramid so tough that a star
   that only glows every one hundred years falls
   into the center giving divine perfect light
I am bad

I sat on the throne
   drinking nectar with allah
I got hot and sent an ice age to europe
   to cool my thirst
My oldest daughter is nefertiti
   the tears from my birth pains
   created the nile
I am a beautiful woman

I gazed on the forest and burned
   out the sahara desert
   with a packet of goat's meat
   and a change of clothes
I crossed it in two hours
I am a gazelle so swift
   so swift you can't catch me

   For a birthday present when he was three
I gave my son hannibal an elephant
   He gave me rome for mother's day
My strength flows ever on

My son noah built new/ark and
I stood proudly at the helm
   as we sailed on a soft summer day

I turned myself into myself and was
    jesus
    men intone my loving name

    All praises All praises
I am the one who would save

I sowed diamonds in my back yard
My bowels deliver uranium
    the filings from my fingernails are
    semi-precious jewels
    On a trip north
I caught a cold and blew
My nose giving oil to the arab world
I am so hip even my errors are correct
I sailed west to reach east and had to round off
    the earth as I went
    The hair from my head thinned and gold was
    laid across three continents

I am so perfect so divine so ethereal so surreal
I cannot be comprehended
    except by my permission

I mean . . . I . . . can fly
    like a bird in the sky . . .

                                    11 may 70

5

for the masai warriors
(of don miller)

remembering my father's drum
remembering the leopard's screetch
if i could weave an ancient rope
and tie myself to history
i'd spring like daylight out of night
into the future of our land
i'd sprint across the grassy plain
and make a nation for the gods
where i could be the man

30 jan. 73

7

poem for flora

when she was little
and colored and ugly with short
straightened hair
and a very pretty smile
she went to sunday school to hear
'bout nebuchadnezzar the king
of the jews

and she would listen

shadrach, meshach and abednego in the fire

and she would learn

how god was neither north
nor south east or west
with no color but all
she remembered was that
Sheba was Black and comely

and she would think

i want to be
like that

1 june 70

9

poem for black boys
(with special love to james)

Where are your heroes, my little Black ones
You are the Indian you so disdainfully shoot
Not the big bad sheriff on his faggoty white horse

You should play run-away-slave
or Mau Mau
These are more in line with your history

Ask your mothers for a Rap Brown gun
Santa just may comply if you wish hard enough
Ask for CULLURD instead of Monopoly
DO NOT SIT IN DO NOT FOLLOW KING
GO DIRECTLY TO STREETS
This is a game you can win

As you sit there with your all understanding eyes
You know the truth of what I'm saying
Play Back-to-Black
Grow a natural and practice vandalism
These are useful games (some say a skill is even
learned)

There is a new game I must tell you of
It's called Catch The Leader Lying
(and knowing your sense of the absurd
you will enjoy this)

Also a company called Revolution has just issued
a special kit for little boys
called Burn Baby
I'm told it has full instructions on how to siphon gas
and fill a bottle

Then our old friend Hide and Seek becomes valid
Because we have much to seek and ourselves to hide
from a lecherous dog

And this poem I give is worth much more
than any nickel bag
or ten cent toy
And you will understand all too soon
That you, my children of battle, are your heroes
You must invent your own games and teach us old
ones how to play

2 april 67

poem for my nephew
(Brother C. B. Soul)

i wish i were
a shadow
oh wow! when they put
the light on
me i'd grow
longer and taller and
BLACKER

25 june 70

intellectualism

sometimes i feel like i just get in
everybody's way
when i was a little girl
i used to go read
or make fudge
when i got bigger i
read
or picked my nose
that's what they called
intelligence
or when i got older
intellectualism
but it was only
that i was in the way

30 april 68

13

knoxville, tennessee

I always like summer
best
you can eat fresh corn
from daddy's garden
and okra
and greens
and cabbage
and lots of
barbecue
and buttermilk
and homemade ice-cream
at the church picnic
and listen to
gospel music
outside
at the church
homecoming
and go to the mountains with
your grandmother
and go barefooted
and be warm
all the time
not only when you go to bed
and sleep

17 may 68

15

nikki-rosa

childhood remembrances are always a drag
if you're Black
you always remember things like living in Woodlawn
with no inside toilet
and if you become famous or something
they never talk about how happy you were to have
your mother
all to yourself and
how good the water felt when you got your bath
from one of those
big tubs that folk in chicago barbecue in
and somehow when you talk about home
it never gets across how much you
understood their feelings
as the whole family attended meetings about
Hollydale
and even though you remember
your biographers never understand
your father's pain as he sells his stock
and another dream goes
And though you're poor it isn't poverty that
concerns you
and though they fought a lot
it isn't your father's drinking that makes any
difference
but only that everybody is together and you
and your sister have happy birthdays and very good
Christmases
and I really hope no white person ever has cause

to write about me
because they never understand
Black love is Black wealth and they'll
probably talk about my hard childhood
and never understand that
all the while I was quite happy

12 april 68

17

a poem for carol
(may she always wear red ribbons)

when i was very little
though it's still true today
there were no sidewalks in lincoln heights
and the home we had on jackson street
was right next to a bus stop and a sewer
which didn't really ever become offensive
but one day from the sewer a little kitten
with one eye gone
came crawling out
though she never really came into our yard but just
sort of hung by to watch the folk
my sister who was always softhearted but able
to act effectively started taking milk
out to her while our father would only say
don't bring *him* home and everyday
after school i would rush home to see if she was still
there and if gary had fed her but i could never
bring myself to go near her
she was so loving
and so hurt and so singularly beautiful and i knew
i had nothing to give that would
replace her one gone eye

and if i had named her which i didn't i'm sure
i would have called her carol

20 dec. 71

alone

i can be
alone by myself
i was
lonely alone
now i'm lonely
with you
something is wrong
there are flies
everywhere
i go

aug. 69

everytime it rains

everytime it rains if its summer
the sky turns pink and the earth smelling
very sweaty calls my feet to play

i usually sit in my chrome kitchen chair
trying to figure how many worms
were drowned and why i didn't for once
go outside naked
        i want to learn
        how to laugh

once i had three plaits and three ribbons
and blue and white seersucker pants
and a lace tee shirt
i grabbed a bunch of grapes and went to find
the end of a rainbow

i walked through the park
up the hill past the vacant lot they just tore down
past the newsstand and the pool hall and still
wasn't there

i remember sitting on the curb in the drizzle

that was funny
but i still didn't laugh

4 march 73

21

word poem
(perhaps worth considering)

as things be/come
let's destroy
then we can destroy
what we be/come
let's build
what we become
when we dream

the funeral of
martin luther king, jr.

His headstone said
FREE AT LAST, FREE AT LAST
But death is a slave's freedom
We seek the freedom of free men
And the construction of a world
Where Martin Luther King could have lived
and preached non-violence

9 april 68

22

beautiful black men
(with compliments and apologies to all not mentioned by name)

i wanta say just gotta say something
bout those beautiful beautiful beautiful outasight
black men
with they afros
walking down the street
is the same ol danger
but a brand new pleasure

sitting on stoops, in bars, going to offices
running numbers, watching for their whores
preaching in churches, driving their hogs
walking their dogs, winking at me
in their fire red, lime green, burnt orange
royal blue tight tight pants that hug
what i like to hug

jerry butler, wilson pickett, the impressions
temptations, mighty mighty sly
don't have to do anything but walk
on stage
and i scream and stamp and shout
see new breed men in breed alls
dashiki suits with shirts that match
the lining that complements the ties
that smile at the sandals
where dirty toes peek at me
and i scream and stamp and shout
for more beautiful beautiful beautiful
black men with outasight afros

10 sept. 68

25

black power
(for all the beautiful
black panthers east)

But the whole thing is a miracle—See?

We were just standing there
talking—not touching or smoking
Pot
When this cop told
Tyrone
Move along buddy—take your whores
outa here

And this tremendous growl
From out of nowhere
Pounced on him

Nobody to this very day
Can explain
How it happened

And none of the zoos or circuses
Within fifty miles
Had reported
A panther
Missing

sept. 68

27

revolutionary dreams

i used to dream militant
dreams of taking
over america to show
these white folks how it should be
done
i used to dream radical dreams
of blowing everyone away with my perceptive
powers
of correct analysis
i even used to think i'd be the one
to stop the riot and negotiate the peace
then i awoke and dug
that if i dreamed natural
dreams of being a natural
woman doing what a woman
does when she's natural
i would have a revolution

20 jan. 70

dreams

in my younger years
before i learned
black people aren't
suppose to dream
i wanted to be
a raelet
and say "dr o wn d in my youn tears"
or "tal kin bout tal kin bout"
or marjorie hendricks and grind
all up against the mic
and scream
"baaaaaby nightandday
baaaaaby nightandday"
then as i grew and matured
i became more sensible
and decided i would
settle down
and just become
a sweet inspiration

2 oct. 68

29

the geni in the jar
(for Nina Simone)

take a note and spin it around spin it around don't
prick your finger
take a note and spin it around
on the Black loom on the Black loom
careful baby
don't prick your finger

take the air and weave the sky
around the Black loom around the Black loom
make the sky sing a Black song sing a blue song
sing my song make the sky sing a Black song
from the Black loom from the Black loom
careful baby
don't prick your finger

take the geni and put her in a jar
put her in a jar
wrap the sky around her
take the geni and put her in a jar
wrap the sky around her
listen to her sing
sing a Black song our Black song
from the Black loom
singing to me
from the Black loom
careful baby
don't prick your finger

17 feb. 70

31

revolutionary music

you've just got to dig sly
and the family stone
forget the words
you gonna be dancing to the music
james brown can go to
viet nam
or sing about whatever he
has to
since he already told
the honkie
"although you happy you better try
to get along
money won't change you
but time is taking you on"
not to mention
doing a whole
song they can't even snap
their fingers to
"good god! ugh!"
talking bout
"i got the feeling baby i got the feeling"
and "hey everybody let me tell you the news"
martha and the vandellas dancing in the streets
while shorty long is functioning at that junction
yeah we hip to that

aretha said they better
think
but she already said
"ain't no way to love you"
(and you know she wasn't talking to us)
and dig the o'jays asking "must i always be a stand
in for love"
i mean they say "i'm a fool for being myself"

While the mighty mighty impressions have told the
world
for once and for all
"We're a Winner"
even our names—le roi has said—are together
impressions
temptations
supremes
delfonics
miracles
intruders (i mean intruders?)
not beatles and animals and white bad things like
young rascals and shit
we be digging all
our revolutionary music consciously or un
cause sam cooke said "a change is gonna come"

april 68

34

communication

if music is the universal language
think of me as one whole note

if science has the most perfect language
just think of me as Mc^2

since mathematics can speak to the infinite
picture me as 1 to the first power

what i mean is one day
i'm gonna grab your love

and you'll be satisfied

29 march 73

35

2nd rapp

they ain't gonna never get
rap
he s a note turned himself
into a million songs listen
to aretha call
his name

he's a light
turned himself into our homes
look how well we see
since he came

he's a spirit turned
pisces to aries
alpha to omega

he's a man
turned himself into Black
women
and we turn little hims
loose on the world

10 march 70